PLACES OF WORSHIP

Synagogues

Sharman Kadish

First published in Great Britain by Heinemann Library
Halley Court, Jordan Hill, Oxford OX2 8EJ
a division of Reed Educational and Professional Publishing Ltd.
Heinemann is a registered trademark of Reed Educational & Professional Publishing Limited.

OXFORD MELBOURNE AUCKLAND
BLANTYRE IBADAN JOHANNESBURG
GABORONE PORTSMOUTH (NH) USA CHICAGO

Designed by Tinstar Design
Illustrations by Nicholas Beresford-Davies and Martin Griffin
Printed by Wing King Tong in Hong Kong

02 01 00 99 98
10 9 8 7 6 5 4 3 2 1

British Library Cataloguing in Publication Data

Kadish, Sharman, 1959-
  Synagogues. - (Places of Worship)
  1. Synagogues - Juvenile literature
  I. Title
  296.6'5

ISBN 0 431 05174 7

Acknowledgements
The Publishers would like to thank the following for permission to reproduce photographs: Andes Press Agency/Carlos Reyes-Manzo, p. 21; Circa Photo Library, p. 12 (left), p.17 (Barrie Searle); Emmett, Phil & Val, pp. 6, 19; Harris, A, p. 15; Hutchison Photo Library, p. 5; Manchester Jewish Museum, pp. 4, 8, 14; Radovan, Zev, pp. 12 (right), 13, 16, 20; Soester, Juliette, p. 7; Stewart, Beverley Jane, p. 9.

Cover photograph reproduced with permission of Juliette Soester. Our thanks to the Lauderdale Road Synagogue of the Spanish and Portuguese Jews' Congregation, London, for allowing us to photograph their synagogue for the front cover.

Our thanks to Philip Emmett for his comments in the preparation of this book, and to Louise Spilsbury for all her hard work. The Author would like to thank Diane Gholam for her comment on the manuscript and Meir Persoff of the Jewish Chronicle.

Every effort has been made to contact copyright holders of any material reproduced in this book. Any omissions will be rectified in subsequent printings if notice is given to the Publisher.

Contents

Words printed in **bold letters like these**
are explained in the Glossary.

What is a synagogue?

A synagogue is the place where Jews meet to **worship God**. Jews follow the religion called **Judaism**. Judaism is one of the oldest religions in the world. Jews believe in one God who created the world.

The name for a synagogue in **Hebrew**, the language of the Jews, is Bet Knesset. The words mean 'house of assembly'.

This synagogue is in Manchester. You can see inside on page 8.

A place to meet

Although Jews can worship anywhere, the synagogue is a special place. In the synagogue, Jews come to pray, study and meet together as a **community**.

To pray inside and outside the synagogue, ten men, called a **minyan**, are all that is needed. The minyan can meet in a private house, in an office, shop or factory, or even in the open air.

A Jew at prayer.

What does it look like?

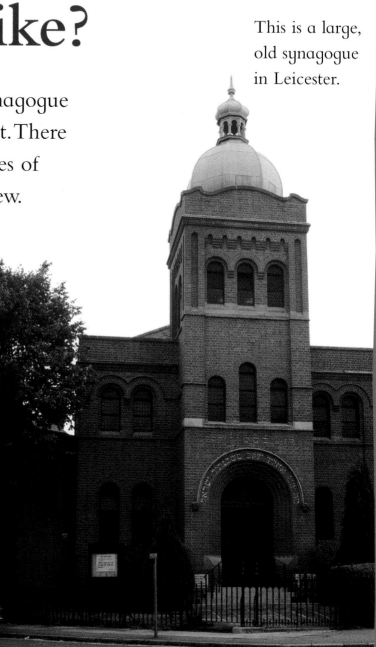

This is a large, old synagogue in Leicester.

From the outside a synagogue may be difficult to spot. There are many different types of synagogues, old and new. Some are large and grand, others are small and plain.

Synagogues are built in all sorts of styles. But they usually have **Hebrew** writing or a Jewish sign, or **symbol**, over the entrance.

This is a
modern
synagogue
in London.

The Hebrew language

Unlike English, which is read from left to right, Hebrew is read from right to left. Hebrew has its own alphabet of 22 letters. The 'Aleph-Bet' is the Hebrew ABC.

The Jewish **Bible** and prayers are written in Hebrew. Jews say their prayers in Hebrew.

This is a piece of Hebrew writing. לִשְׁמוֹעַ לִלְמוֹד

What's inside?

When you go into the synagogue you walk through an outer room, or vestibule, to reach the prayer hall. Inside, the prayer hall may be very simple, or decorated with marble and gold, and coloured glass windows. You hardly ever see pictures or statues of people or animals. This is because Jews are not allowed to make any **images** of living things, which they might start to **worship** instead of the one true **God**.

This is the inside of the synagogue on page 4. Can you see the **Hebrew** writing above the window?

The women's section

According to Jewish tradition, men and boys
sit away from women and girls in the synagogue.
Sometimes the women and girls sit behind a
screen at the back
of the hall. In big
synagogues there
is a ladies' gallery
(Ezrat Nashim)
upstairs. Men,
boys and married
women cover
their heads.

In this painting
you can see
women sitting
upstairs in a
synagogue.

The Ark and the bimah

The **Ark** is the most important piece of furniture in the synagogue. Usually, it looks like a big wardrobe. The **scrolls** which are kept inside the Ark are the most precious objects in the synagogue. A beautiful curtain (parohet) covers the scrolls. Above the Ark hangs a special lamp (ner tamid) which is lit all the time.

Usually, the Ark is on the wall facing Jerusalem, the **Holy** City. Jerusalem is to the south-east of Britain. Jews pray facing towards Jerusalem.

This Ark is 300 years old. It is in a synagogue in London which is the oldest synagogue in Britain.

The bimah

In the middle of the prayer hall you will see
a small stage on which there is a reading
desk. This is the **bimah** or **tevah**. The **Torah**
is read from here during some **services**.

Most synagogues are designed from a plan like this one.

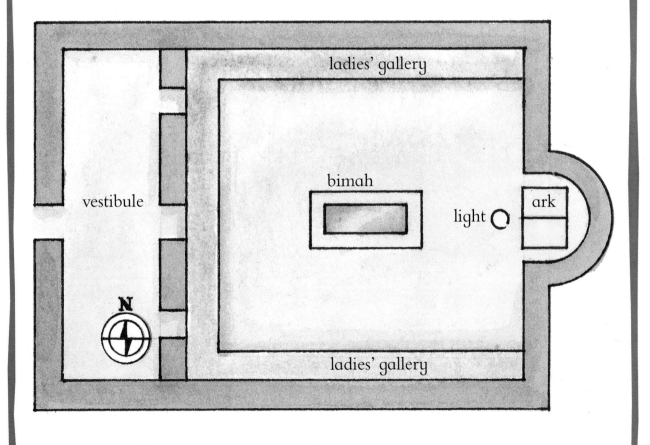

The Torah scroll

A **scroll** (**Sefer Torah**) is taken out of the **Ark** during some **services**. A scroll is like a book but it is handwritten on one very long page and rolled up. The first five books of the Jewish **Bible** (the **Torah**) are written in **Hebrew** on the scrolls. The Torah is the most important Jewish **holy** book. It tells the Jewish people how **God** wants them to live.

The scroll is protected inside a beautiful cover. This is usually made of fine fabric sewn with gold thread. Sometimes the scroll is kept inside a wooden case covered with silver.

Two Torah scrolls

Often a silver shield and a rod, called a **yad**, hang over the cover. Silver crowns or bells decorate the handles. The bells tinkle as the Torah is being carried in the synagogue.

Bar Mitzvah

When a Jewish boy is 13 years old he becomes **Bar Mitzvah**. He is called up to the **bimah** to read from the Torah scroll. He is counted as a grown-up and he must obey all of the **mitzvot** (**commandments**) given in the Torah.

A Bar Mitzvah boy reading from the Torah. He is wearing a special prayer shawl (tallit) and a small cap, or skull cap (kippah) on his head.

Things to look for

There are several things to look out for inside and outside a synagogue. See if you can spot some **Hebrew** words above the entrance door or above the **Ark**. They remind Jews of the tablets of stone on which the Ten **Commandments** were first written. These are the basic laws which tell Jews how to live.

You may also see two columns, one on each side of the synagogue entrance or the Ark. The pillars remind Jews of the **Temple**, which also had grand columns.

The stone tablets with Hebrew writing on them. The words stand for the Ten Commandments.

The kind of pillars you may see in a synagogue.

Other symbols to see

Sometimes you will see a candlestick with seven branches. It is called a **menorah**. It reminds Jews of the Menorah which stood in the Temple in Jerusalem.

You may see a star with six points. It is called the Magen David or the 'Shield of David', the Jewish Star of David. David was one of the most famous kings in Jewish history.

Can you see the Star of David, the menorah and the tablets of stone in this colourful synagogue window?

What happens there?

There are prayers in the synagogue three times every day, and also on festivals and on **Shabbat**. Shabbat is the Jewish **holy** day, a special day of rest and **worship**. It begins on Friday at sunset and lasts until Saturday nightfall.

Many synagogues have a **rabbi**. He often leads the prayers. His main job is to teach the family, especially the children, about their religion.

Children learning about the Jewish religion.

Some big synagogues have a **hazan**. He stands on the **bimah** and sings the prayers. Sometimes there is also a choir. No musical instruments are played in the synagogue, except perhaps at weddings.

Weddings

Weddings often take place in the synagogue. The bride and groom stand under a special wedding canopy called a huppah. The huppah is a sign of the home they will share.

A Jewish bride and groom standing under the huppah (wedding canopy).

17

The First Temple

There have been Jews for over 4000 years. Jews believe that they should know all about their past. The **Bible** tells us that the Jewish people lived in the desert for 40 years after they left Egypt. In those days the Jewish people were called the Children of **Israel** or the **Hebrews**. Moses, their great leader and teacher, was given the **Torah** by **God** on Mount Sinai. In the Torah was the **commandment** to build a **holy** place where the Hebrews could pray to God.

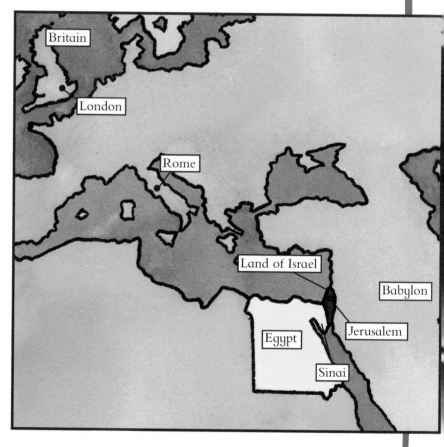

This map shows all of the places you learn about on these two pages, and the next.

Building the Temple

First of all the Children of Israel built a simple holy place, the **Mishkan**, which was like a tent. It could be packed up and moved from place to place. When they finally settled in the Land of Israel, King Solomon built a splendid temple there. This was the Holy **Temple** (Bet HaMikdash) of Jerusalem.

The Temple was the most important place of **worship** for the Jews. Today, wherever Jews pray, they stand facing towards Jerusalem.

This is a model of how the Temple in Jerusalem probably looked.

What the Temple means today

Solomon's **Temple** was destroyed when the Land of **Israel** was conquered by soldiers from the country of Babylon. The Jews were sent away to Babylon.

When the Jews returned, they rebuilt the Temple in Jerusalem. King Herod's Temple was even bigger and more beautiful than the first. Sadly, the Second Temple was burnt by the Roman army when they conquered Jerusalem.

The Romans stole the **Menorah** from the Temple in Jerusalem and carried it back to Rome. You will see **menorot** in synagogues today.

The Western Wall

Today, all that is left of the Temple is one wall. It is called the Western Wall. Jews from all over the world go to Jerusalem to pray at the Western Wall, their most important **holy** place.

In synagogues everywhere you will find reminders of the Temple in Jerusalem. Jews believe the Temple will be rebuilt when the **Messiah** comes.

Jewish women praying at the Western Wall in Jerusalem.

Glossary

Ark place in the synagogue where the Torah scrolls are kept

Bar Mitzvah ceremony which takes place when a Jewish boy is 13 years old. Bar Mitzvah means 'son of the commandments.'

Bible the Hebrew Bible is the Jewish holy book

bimah platform with reading desk in the synagogue

Commandments the laws given by God to the Jewish people. These laws are called the mitzvot in Hebrew.

community group of people who share the same beliefs and who pray together in the same way

God Jews believe that there is only one God who created the world

hazan singer who sometimes leads the synagogue service

Hebrew the Jewish holy language

Hebrews in Bible times the Jewish people were called Hebrews or the Children of Israel

holy means special because it is to do with God

images pictures or models of people, animals or objects

Israel the Jewish people and land

Judaism the religion of the Jews, people who are Jewish. Judaism is one of the oldest religions in the world.

Menorah the candlestick with seven branches which stood in the Temple in Jerusalem. Today the menorah is often shown with nine branches. (**menorot**: more than one menorah).

Messiah a member of the family of King David who will one day come to rebuild the Temple and bring peace to the world

minyan the ten men needed to hold Jewish prayers

Mishkan the tent in the desert made by the Children of Israel where they prayed to God

mitzvot see Commandments

rabbi Jewish teacher

scroll rolled-up 'book'

Sefer Torah rolled-up book or scroll on which the Torah is written by hand in Hebrew

service special meeting for worship

Shabbat the Jewish day of rest and worship. It lasts from sunset on Friday to nightfall on Saturday.

symbol a sign with a special meaning

Temple the Jewish house of worship in Jerusalem which was destroyed 2000 years ago. It is called Bet HaMikdash in Hebrew.

tevah another name for the bimah

Torah the first five books of the Jewish Bible. The word Torah is also used to mean the whole of Jewish teaching.

worship to show respect and love for God, usually through prayer

yad a silver rod or pointer used to keep the place when reading from the Torah scroll. It is called a yad or 'hand' in Hebrew because it is made with a small hand with a pointing finger at its end.

Index